ANCIENT EGYPT

BY GEORGE COTTRELL

KidHaven
PUBLISHING

Published in 2017 by
KidHaven Publishing, an Imprint of Greenhaven Publishing, LLC
353 3rd Avenue
Suite 255
New York, NY 10010

© 2017 Booklife Publishing
This edition is published by arrangement with Booklife Publishing

Designer: Natalie Carr
Editor: Grace Jones

Cataloging-in-Publication Data

Names: Cottrell, George.
Title: Ancient Egypt / George Cottrell.
Description: New York : KidHaven Publishing, 2017. | Series: Unlocking ancient civilizations | Includes index.
Identifiers: ISBN 9781534520257 (pbk.) | ISBN 9781534520271 (library bound) | ISBN 9781534520264 (6 pack) | ISBN 9781534520288 (ebook)
Subjects: LCSH: Egypt–Civilization–To 332 B.C.–Juvenile literature.
Classification: LCC DT61.C68 2017 | DDC 932–dc23

Printed in the United States of America

CPSIA compliance information: Batch #CW17KL: For further information contact Greenhaven Publishing LLC, New York, New York at 1-844-317-7404.

Please visit our website, www.greenhavenpublishing.com. For a free color catalog of all our high-quality books, call toll free 1-844-317-7404 or fax 1-844-317-7405.

PHOTO CREDITS

Abbreviations: l–left, r–right, b–bottom, t–top, c–center, m–middle.
Front Coverm – Jaroslav Moravcik. Front Cover Background – Fedor Selivanov. 2 – Dudarev Mikhail. 4t – Evgeny Sayfutdinov. 4bl – JJ_SNIPER. 5b – Ignatius Tan. 6 – Waj. 7ml – Jose Ignacio Soto. 7b – Andrey_Popov. 8t – Kekyalyaynen. 8bl – tan_tan. 9tr – Matej Hudovernik. 9bl – Jaroslav Moravcik. 10 – Matej Kastelic. 11b – WitR. 12m – Boonsom. 12bl – Jane Rix. 12-13m – garanga. 13br – Pius Lee. 14t – erichon. 14br – Taigi. 15b – ArtMari. 15t – Morphart Creation. 16bl – mountainpix. 17 background – Fedor Selivanov. 17r – tkachuk. 18t – Kamira. 18bl – Fedor Selivanov. 19tr – Vladimir Korostyshevskiy. 19b – PerseoMedusa. 20bl – tan_tan. 20r – BasPhoto. 21t – Ashwin. 21b – Stephen Chung. 22t – andersphoto. 22bl – Photography (c) 2002 Zubro and released under GFDL, via wikicommons. 23 – Giancarlo Liguori. 24 – Anastasios71. 25ml – mishabender. 25mr – mishabender. 26 -Tawfik Dajani. 27t – Tawfik Dajani. 27b – FreeProd33. 28tl – erichon. 28tm – givaga. 28tr – Waj. 28bl – meunierd. 28bm – mountainpix. 29tl – WitR. 29tm – suronin. 29tr – Ignatius Tan. 29bm – Classical Numismatic Group, Inc. http://www.cngcoins.com [GFDL (http://www.gnu.org/copyleft/fdl.html), CC-BY-SA-3.0 (http://creativecommons.org/licenses/by-sa/3.0/) or CC BY-SA 2.5 (http://creativecommons.org/licenses/by-sa/2.5)], via Wikimedia Commons. 29br – Anton_Ivanov. Images are courtesy of Shutterstock.com. With thanks to Getty Images, Thinkstock Photo and iStockphoto.

ANCIENT EGYPT

CONTENTS

All words that appear like *this* are explained in the glossary on page 31.

THE ANCIENT EGYPTIANS

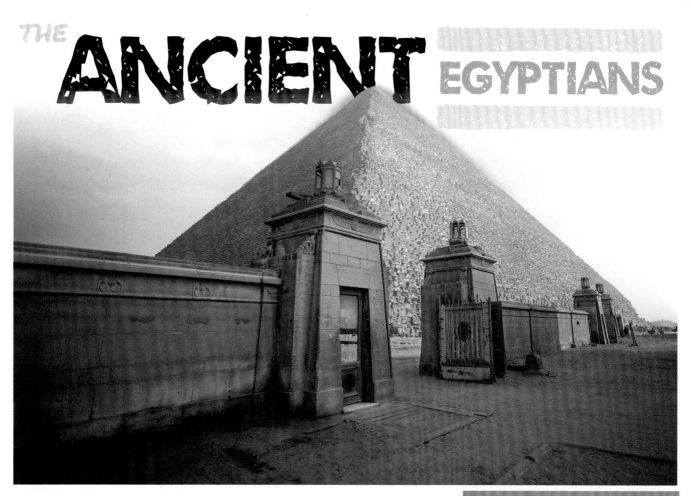

THE BEGINNINGS OF ANCIENT EGYPT

OVER 7,000 years ago, the *civilization* of ancient Egypt began along the banks of the Nile River in what is now modern-day Egypt. It was one of the world's first civilizations and also one of the most well-known and impressive. The civilization lasted for more than 3,000 years and is one of the longest-lasting civilizations in human history.

Ancient Egypt first began around 3500 BC, when people started to settle near the Nile River because of the *fertile* farming land found around its banks and the easy access to water it provided. Over time, these first settlers created two kingdoms: Lower Egypt and Upper Egypt, which were ruled by different *tribes*. In around 3100 BC, these two kingdoms were joined together by the pharaoh Menes in the first Egyptian dynasty—Dynasty I.

THE THREE KINGDOMS OF EGYPT

Historians usually group the history of ancient Egypt into three major kingdoms: the Old Kingdom, the Middle Kingdom, and the New Kingdom. It was during these times that ancient Egypt was united and at its strongest, both financially and culturally. Dynasties were periods of time when leaders from the same family ruled.

THE OLD KINGDOM (2686–2180 BC)

The year 2686 BC was the beginning of what is now known as the Old Kingdom. It was during this time that ancient Egypt began to succeed and grow. The country was united, had a strong government, and had begun to trade with other countries and civilizations.

Some *historians* call the Old Kingdom "The Age of the Pyramids." This is because the first ever pyramid was built during this period. As well as this, the Great Pyramid of Giza and the remarkable statue, the Great Sphinx of Giza, were also built during this time. These remarkable pyramid structures were built as tombs for the rulers of ancient Egypt. The Old Kingdom was also when Egyptian art began to be produced. The styles of the Old Kingdom's art would be copied for thousands of years.

THE GREAT SPHINX AND THE PYRAMID OF KHAFRE, THE SECOND-LARGEST PYRAMID EVER BUILT

THE MIDDLE KINGDOM (1975 BC–1640 BC)

After a period when Egypt suffered from repeated droughts and famines, the Old Kingdom collapsed. During this time there was no government and it was a time of social unrest and chaos. This period is now known as the First Intermediate Period and lasted for around 150 years.

Eventually, in 1975 BC, a pharaoh known as Mentuhotep II reunited Egypt under one ruler. This was the start of the Middle Kingdom.

Again, ancient Egypt grew wealthy and began to extend its influence. Also, Thebes became its capital city and would remain an important political and religious center, while the pharaohs of the time created a powerful army to protect Egypt.

THE RUINS AT LUXOR, THE MODERN-DAY CITY IN EGYPT WHERE THEBES USED TO BE

THE NEW KINGDOM (1520 BC–1075 BC)

After the Middle Kingdom, Egypt yet again became divided. This was because ancient Egypt was invaded by a foreign people called the Hyksos who came from Western Asia.

The Hyksos were fierce warriors and introduced the horse and chariot to Egypt. However, a young pharaoh known as Ahmose I defeated the Hyksos and reunited Egypt once again.

This marked the beginning of the New Kingdom, the time when ancient Egypt was at its most powerful and the last great period of the civilization. During the New Kingdom many lands were *conquered*, such as Israel, Lebanon, and Syria, while trading with foreigners increased and brought wealth and luxury goods, such as *myrrh*, into Egypt. The New Kingdom is known for its famous and powerful pharaohs such as Ramses II and Tutankhamun, and burial sites like the Valley of the Kings.

THIS ANCIENT EGYPTIAN HORSE-DRAWN CHARIOT WOULD HAVE BEEN MADE AFTER THE INVASION OF THE HYKSOS.

THIS IS THE GREAT TEMPLE OF HATSHEPSUT IN THE VALLEY OF THE KINGS. HATSHEPSUT WAS ONE OF TWO FEMALE LEADERS OF THE NEW KINGDOM.

THE PHARAOHS

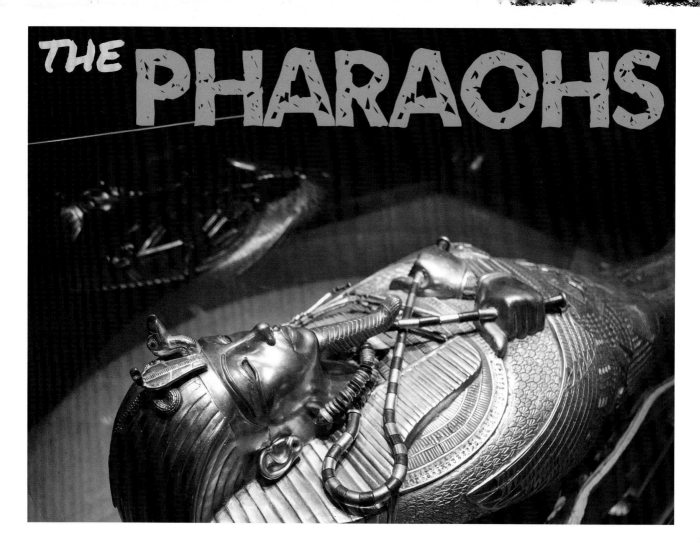

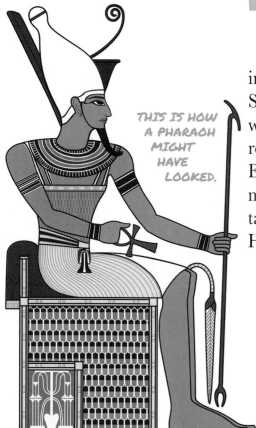

THIS IS HOW A PHARAOH MIGHT HAVE LOOKED.

THE pharaoh was the most important and powerful person in Egyptian **society**. Similar to a king, they were the political and religious leaders of the Egyptian people and, normally, only males could take the title of pharaoh. However, occasionally women became pharaohs as well. Some of the most well-known pharaohs, such as Cleopatra and Hatshepsut, were women. They were normally chosen because they were the nearest living **descendants** of the previous pharaohs.

During the civilization, there were over 170 pharaohs that ruled over the kingdom. They owned all of the land of Egypt, made laws, collected *taxes* and helped both to protect ancient Egypt and conquer new lands and people.

The people of Egypt believed that a pharaoh was half-man, half-god and could speak to the gods. They thought that each pharaoh was the god Horus, a god of the sky. It was because of this that they thought the pharaohs had such power. While most of the pharaohs had many wives, there was always only one queen.

The burials of pharaohs were very important. Pyramids were built as impressive tombs for them to make sure that they were protected on their journey to the *afterlife*. In the New Kingdom, pharaohs were buried in the Valley of the Kings at Thebes. Instead of pyramids, these tombs were tunnels carved deep into rock.

THIS IS THE MASK OF TUTANKHAMUN. MADE IN THE IMAGE OF THE PHARAOH, IT WAS FOUND IN HIS TOMB.

TUTANKHAMUN (1341 BC–1323 BC)

Tutankhamun is perhaps the most famous of all of the pharaohs. This is because his tomb was found in 1922 and contained treasures and *artifacts* that were unlike any others previously discovered. It allowed historians to learn many things about him, such as the fact that he became pharaoh at just seven years old.

THE PYRAMIDS AND EGYPTIAN BUILDINGS

O F all of the things ancient Egypt is known for, the pyramids are perhaps the most famous. First built during the Old Kingdom as tombs and **monuments** for the pharaohs, they are some of the most impressive structures built by humans during ancient times and many still survive to this day.

The very first pyramids are called step pyramids. They have large ledges up the sides that look like steps. Historians believe these were put there to help the pharaohs climb towards the sun god, Ra. Pyramids that were built later had flat, sloping sides. This style was supposed to represent the sun's rays.

THE GREAT PYRAMID OF GIZA

The largest of all the pyramids is the Great Pyramid of Giza. When it was first built it was 479 feet (146 meters) tall. The entire structure covers over 550,000 square feet (52,000 square meters) and is made up of 2.3 million stone blocks.

Historians believe that it took over 20,000 workers over 20 years to build the Great Pyramid of Giza. Finished in around 2560 BC, it was the tallest man-made structure in the world for more than 3,800 years.

HOW WERE THE PYRAMIDS BUILT?

Building a pyramid started with planning. The ancient Egyptians developed methods of measurement and used math to make sure that they would not collapse. Then, stone from quarries would be dragged on sledges or brought down the Nile by boat to the site of the pyramid.

THIS IS A VIEW OF THE PYRAMIDS AT GIZA.
THE GREAT PYRAMID OF GIZA IS IN THE MIDDLE.

As the ancient Egyptians had no cranes or modern building equipment, historians believe that the workers would have cut up the stone into blocks and then moved them up the pyramid on a mud-and-brick ramp one at a time.

THIS IS HOW THE LIGHTHOUSE OF ALEXANDRIA MIGHT HAVE LOOKED.

WHAT WAS INSIDE?

In the very center would be the pharaoh's *burial chamber*. Due to the length of time it took to build a pyramid, pharaohs would start building a pyramid as soon as they came to power to make sure it was finished by the time they died. The burial chamber would be filled with treasure and other items of the pharaoh. Smaller rooms would surround the chamber, where his relatives and servants would also be buried.

A STAIRCASE TO A TOMB IN A STEP PYRAMID

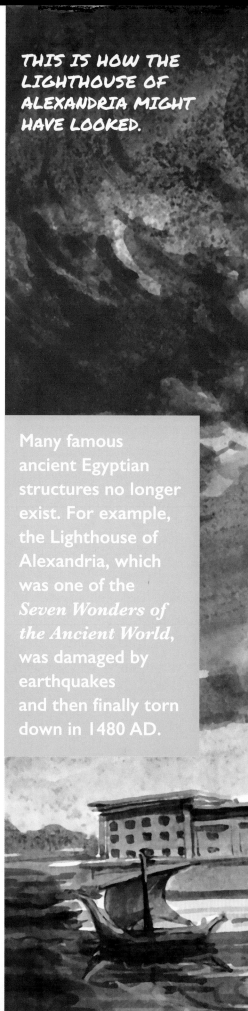

Many famous ancient Egyptian structures no longer exist. For example, the Lighthouse of Alexandria, which was one of the *Seven Wonders of the Ancient World*, was damaged by earthquakes and then finally torn down in 1480 AD.

THE CLOSE-UP OF A PYRAMID AT GIZA CLEARLY SHOWS THE STONE BLOCKS THAT MAKE UP THE PYRAMID.

OTHER GREAT EGYPTIAN STRUCTURES

The pyramids were not the only impressive structures that the ancient Egyptians built. One other example is the Great Sphinx of Giza. A sphinx was a **mythological** creature with the body of a lion and head of a person.

The Egyptians built statues of them to guard important locations. The Great Sphinx of Giza guards the pyramids and tombs at Giza and is very large—262 feet (80 meters) long, 23 feet (7 meters) wide, and 72 feet (22 meters) high!

THE GREAT SPHINX OF GIZA

EVERYDAY LIFE

THIS IS THE NILE AS IT LOOKS TODAY. THIS PICTURE SHOWS JUST HOW FERTILE THE BANKS OF THE RIVER ARE.

EVERYDAY life in ancient Egypt was centered around the Nile River. Each year the Nile would flood and make the soil fertile, which would bring good harvests and wealth to the kingdom.

Many of the **peasants** were farmers. They grew crops such as barley to make beer, vegetables to eat, and **flax** to make into linen for clothes.

The clothes worn by ancient Egyptians were very simple and usually white in color so they could try to keep cool in the hot weather conditions. Both men and women wore makeup—normally blue and green eyeshadow and black eyeliner. Almost everyone, whether rich or poor, wore pieces of jewelry including *amulets*, which they believed protected the wearer.

AN EGYPTIAN AMULET MADE OF METAL AND PRECIOUS STONES

ANCIENT EGYPTIAN HOMES

The ancient Egyptians were skilled builders and craftsmen, and they built many types of homes. Peasants and farmers would have usually lived in small villages and their homes would have been built using easily available materials, such as bricks made out of mud. Houses in towns and cities would have been much more *cramped* and close together in small streets due to larger, denser populations.

A DRAWING OF WHAT AN EGYPTIAN HOME WOULD HAVE LOOKED LIKE

Wealthy ancient Egyptians would have lived in villas, often in the countryside. These villas would have had many rooms, including servants' quarters, and beautiful gardens surrounded by walls. The villas would have contained expensive furniture made out of wood or even rarer materials such as ebony—a rare, expensive dark wood—decorated with precious stones.

HOW WAS SOCIETY DIVIDED?

Ancient Egyptian society was divided into a clear *hierarchy*. At the very top was the pharaoh, followed by the royal family. After this came the upper classes, which included nobles, landowners, and members of the government.

Those with professions such as merchants and craftsmen came next, followed by the lower classes who made up the majority of ancient Egypt, who were farmers and peasants. The lowest of all were the slaves.

WOMEN IN SOCIETY

Unlike many other ancient civilizations, women in ancient Egypt were treated well and had a lot of the same rights that men had. For example, women were allowed to own property. Women also worked in jobs as nurses, gardeners, and entertainers. Women from wealthy backgrounds could even become *priestesses* and doctors.

HIERARCHY

1. PHARAOH

2. ROYAL FAMILY

3. UPPER CLASSES

4. LOWER CLASSES

5. SLAVES

ART AND CULTURE

Much of what we know about ancient Egypt has been learned through the art that has been discovered. Art and culture were a big part of ancient Egyptian life and were used mainly to show the stories of the gods and the pharaohs.

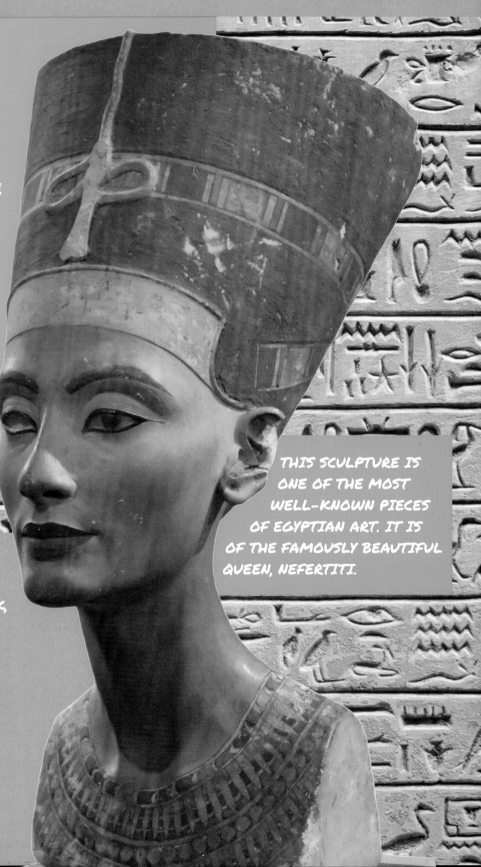

Some of the most common types of art in ancient Egypt were the paintings on the walls of the tombs of Egyptians. These paintings would show the person passing into the afterlife or scenes from their actual life. As well as their giant statues, such as the Sphinx, Egyptians also carved smaller, more delicate sculptures. They made these from materials such as ivory, limestone, and sometimes even gold.

THIS SCULPTURE IS ONE OF THE MOST WELL-KNOWN PIECES OF EGYPTIAN ART. IT IS OF THE FAMOUSLY BEAUTIFUL QUEEN, NEFERTITI.

WHEN PAINTING, THE EGYPTIANS NORMALLY ONLY USED BLUE, BLACK, RED, GREEN AND GOLD AS COLORS.

LANGUAGE AND WRITING

THE Egyptians first started to use hieroglyphics in about 3000 BC, when they would have been carved or painted onto stone. However, they were only used in special places or for important events, such as tombs, temples and religious ceremonies. For day-to-day writing, the Egyptians used a type of writing called Hieratic that was much more simple.

HIEROGLYPHICS

Hieroglyphics were the ancient Egyptians' formal system of writing. Instead of letters, the system used pictures of objects, people, and animals called hieroglyphs. Each picture would represent either a sound, a word, or an object. Hieroglyphs can be read in any direction.

HIEROGLYPHS CARVED INTO STONE

THE ROSETTA STONE

The Rosetta Stone is a large stone slab that has helped historians understand hieroglyphics. Discovered in 1799, it features the same piece of writing in three different languages: Egyptian hieroglyphs, Demotic script and ancient Greek. In 1822, Jean-François Champollion finally discovered how hieroglyphics could be read by comparing the three languages on the Rosetta Stone. It was the first time in over 1,400 years that they could be understood.

THE ROSETTA STONE

PAPYRUS

This is the *Book of the Dead*, an important ancient Egyptian piece of writing. It contains spells that are supposed to help the dead reach the afterlife. It is written on papyrus.

Papyrus is a paper-like material that the Egyptians used to write on. The ancient Egyptians were the first civilization to use papyrus and they made it from the papyrus plant that grew in large numbers by the Nile River. They often created large scrolls from it and used them to record important information or events. Before they invented papyrus, the Egyptians used to carve or paint their writing onto stone.

GODS AND GODDESSES

RELIGION played a central role in the life of the ancient Egyptians. They worshipped many gods and goddesses who represented different aspects of the world and their daily lives. For instance, Tefnut was the goddess of the rain and Sekhmet was the goddess of war. Pharaohs would build large temples in honor of gods and goddesses and towns would have their own temples. Egyptian people believed that gods and goddesses could live in temples while they were on Earth.

THIS WAS WHAT THE ANCIENT EGYPTIANS THOUGHT THE GOD HORUS LOOKED LIKE.

In the temple, priests and priestesses would say prayers and sing hymns to try to please the gods and goddesses. Each temple would have a statue dedicated to whichever god or goddess the temple was built for.

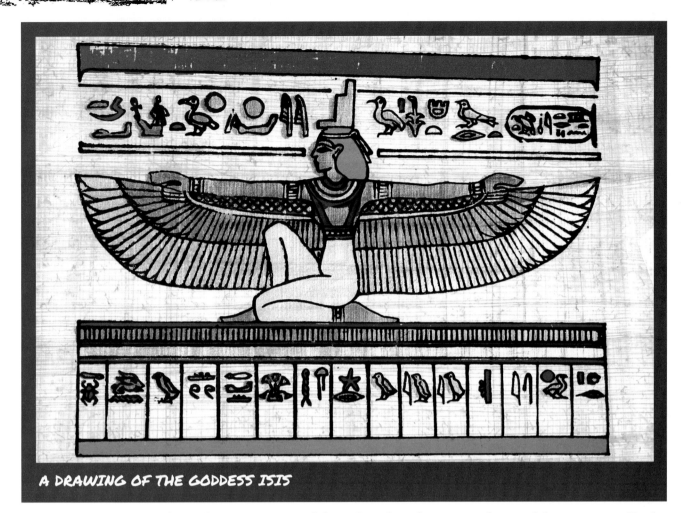

A DRAWING OF THE GODDESS ISIS

The Egyptians believed in a wide variety of gods and goddesses and viewed some as more important than others. For instance, the god Ra was considered to be the most important god of them all. He was believed to be the sun god and the supreme ruler of all of the other gods. The main goddess was called Isis. She was seen as the protector of all.

Egyptians also thought that many kinds of animal were sacred. They believed that certain gods and goddesses would take the form of an animal when coming down to Earth. Cats were thought of as one of the most sacred animals because they represented the goddess Bastet. Due to this, they were often buried and placed in tombs alongside humans.

BURIAL CUSTOMS

A MUMMY AND ITS SARCOPHAGUS

THE ancient Egyptians believed that if a body was **preserved** after death, it would help the body to reach the afterlife and achieve **immortality**. Although these rituals were often only available to the very wealthy due to their cost, they played an important role for everyone in Egyptian society.

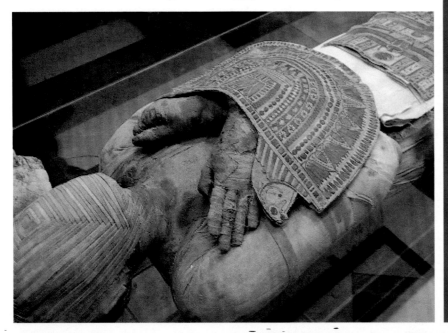

To make sure that the bodies of the dead survived the journey to the afterlife, the ancient Egyptians developed the process of mummification. Mummification made sure that the bodies did not rot and remained well-preserved for thousands of years. The bodies that underwent this process are called mummies. Many of the mummies found by archaeologists in recent years have barely changed since they were buried thanks to this process.

THE PROCESS OF MUMMIFICATION

The first step of mummification was to remove certain organs from the body, such as the brain, liver, lungs, and intestines. The heart was left in place and salt crystals were inserted into the body in order to dry it out. This was very important to make sure that the body did not rot. The body was then wrapped in linen and placed in a stone coffin known as a sarcophagus.

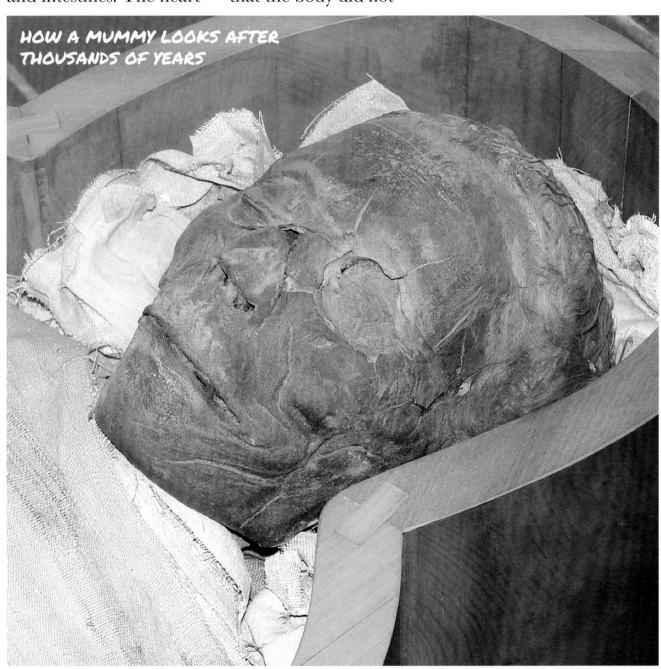

HOW A MUMMY LOOKS AFTER THOUSANDS OF YEARS

In the tomb, alongside the sarcophagus, the Egyptians would place different types of items that they thought might be needed by the dead in the afterlife, such as clothes, food, and furniture. Scenes from the dead person's life would be painted on the walls of their tomb to celebrate their life.

THE END OF ANCIENT EGYPT

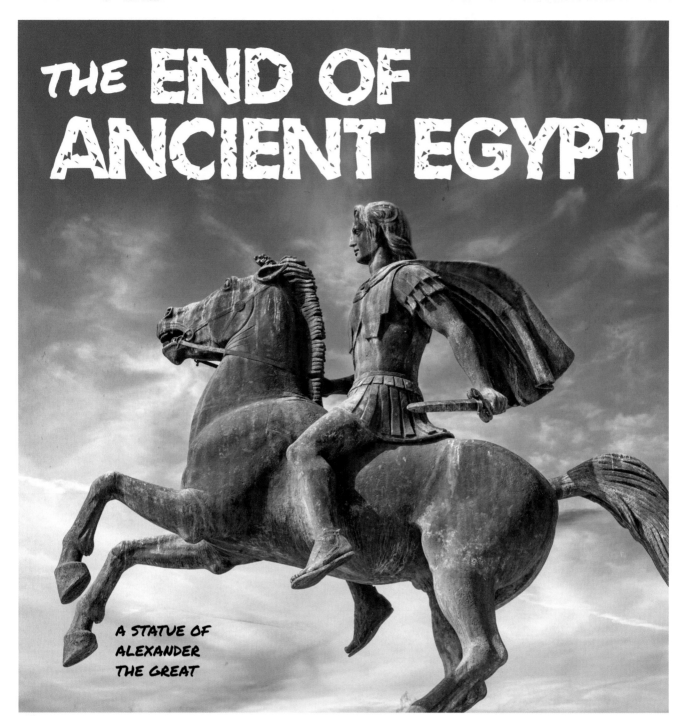

A STATUE OF ALEXANDER THE GREAT

IN around 525 BC the Persians, led by King Cambyses II, invaded Egypt. Egypt then became part of the Persian Empire—the largest empire in the world at the time. The Persians would rule over Egypt for roughly 200 years until 332 BC, when Alexander the Great defeated the Persians.

The Late Period—which was around 664 BC to 332 BC—marked the decline of the great civilization. When the Late Period started, ancient Egypt was still led by Egyptians who ruled for around 125 years as the 26th Dynasty. They tried to re-establish many old traditions, such as building monuments to the gods. However, this was not to last.

THE PTOLEMAIC DYNASTY

When Alexander the Great died, his general, Ptolemy, took control of Egypt and began the Ptolemaic Dynasty. Ruling for over 250 years, this was to be the last Egyptian dynasty. At first, the dynasty was successful, but poor leadership in later years led to the Egyptian people becoming unhappy with the dynasty.

MARCUS ANTONIUS

CLEOPATRA VII

ANTONY AND CLEOPATRA ARE TWO OF THE MOST FAMOUS PEOPLE IN ANCIENT EGYPTIAN HISTORY. SHAKESPEARE EVEN WROTE A PLAY ABOUT THEM.

ANTONY AND CLEOPATRA - THE END OF ANCIENT EGYPT

Cleopatra VII was the last ruler of the Ptolemaic dynasty. She and her husband, Mark Antony the Roman, tried to protect Egypt, but in 31 BC the Egyptians were defeated at the Battle of Actium by the Romans. This was the end of ancient Egypt. The region then became part of the Roman Empire, where it would remain for more than 600 years.

THE LEGACY OF THE ANCIENT EGYPTIANS

AS ancient Egypt was one of the first ancient civilizations to form in the world, as well as being one of the most advanced, many of their technologies had a lasting influence. Some of their inventions are still used today!

IRRIGATION DITCHES LIKE THIS ONE ARE STILL USED EVEN TODAY.

One Egyptian invention that we still use today is the toothbrush. Most Egyptians had a diet consisting mainly of tough bread, which meant that it was important for them to keep their teeth healthy and strong. They used to make their toothpaste out of ash, eggshells and even ground-up ox hooves! Modern-day Egyptian life is still focused around the Nile, and the land surrounding it is still divided by *irrigation ditches*, similar to the ones the ancient Egyptians created.

The achievements of the ancient Egyptians were so impressive, especially for a civilization that existed so long ago, that people all around the world still visit what remains of ancient Egypt. Ancient Egyptian art and artifacts are in most of the world's major museums, and millions of people visit the pyramids every year. People also regularly visit the sites of other famous surviving Egyptian monuments, such as the Great Sphinx and the Valley of the Kings.

THE VALLEY OF THE KINGS

TOURISTS COME TO EGYPT IN THE MILLIONS TO SEE ANCIENT EGYPT'S MOST FAMOUS SITES.

Thanks to the hot and dry climate in Egypt that helps to preserve buildings, as well as the efforts of historians and archaeologists to protect ancient Egyptian sites in recent years, a very large amount of the legacy of ancient Egypt has survived and will continue to be preserved. This will allow us to marvel at the achievements of the ancient Egyptians for many more years to come!

 # TIMELINE OF THE

3500 BC

THE FIRST SETTLERS ARRIVE IN THE NILE VALLEY

3100 BC

UPPER AND LOWER EGYPT ARE UNITED AND WHAT WE KNOW AS ANCIENT EGYPT BEGINS

2686 BC

THE OLD KINGDOM BEGINS

1479 - 1458 BC

THE REIGN OF HATSHEPSUT

1333 - 1323 BC

THE REIGN OF TUTANKHAMUN

1279 - 1213 BC

THE REIGN OF RAMSES II

664 BC

THE LATE PERIOD BEGINS

ANCIENT EGYPTIANS

2560 BC

THE GREAT PYRAMID AT GIZA IS COMPLETED

1975 BC

THE MIDDLE KINGDOM BEGINS

1520 BC

THE NEW KINGDOM BEGINS

525 BC

THE PERSIANS INVADE ANCIENT EGYPT

332 BC

EGYPT IS CONQUERED BY ALEXANDER THE GREAT

205 - 180 BC

THE REIGN OF PTOLEMY V

31 BC

THE EGYPTIANS ARE DEFEATED AT THE BATTLE OF ACTIUM, WHICH BRINGS ABOUT THE END OF ANCIENT EGYPT

MAP OF ANCIENT EGYPT

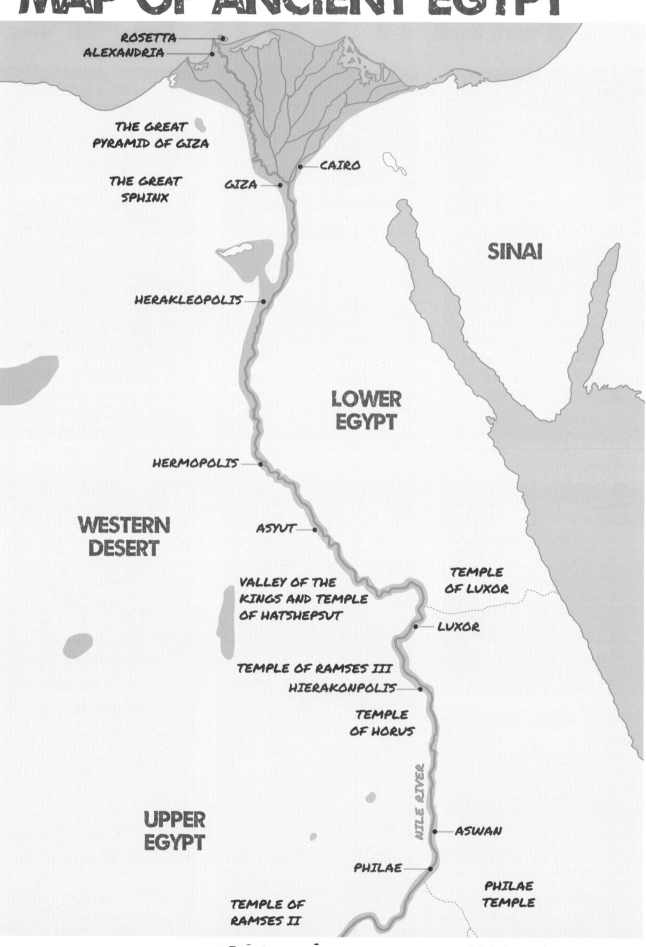

ROSETTA
ALEXANDRIA

THE GREAT
PYRAMID OF GIZA

CAIRO

THE GREAT
SPHINX

GIZA

SINAI

HERAKLEOPOLIS

LOWER
EGYPT

HERMOPOLIS

WESTERN
DESERT

ASYUT

TEMPLE
OF LUXOR

VALLEY OF THE
KINGS AND TEMPLE
OF HATSHEPSUT

LUXOR

TEMPLE OF RAMSES III
HIERAKONPOLIS

TEMPLE
OF HORUS

NILE RIVER

UPPER
EGYPT

ASWAN

PHILAE

PHILAE
TEMPLE

TEMPLE OF
RAMSES II

GLOSSARY

afterlife	a religious belief that there is life after death
amulets	pieces of jewelry thought to protect the wearer against evil, danger, or disease
artifacts	objects made by people, typically ones of cultural or historical interest
burial chamber	a closed space or room where people can be buried once they have died
civilization	a society that is very advanced
conquered	to have overcome or taken control of something by force
cramped	uncomfortably small
descendants	people who have descended from others, usually family members of some significance
fertile	land that is easy to grow plants and crops on
flax	a plant that can be farmed for food or to make linen
hierarchy	a system where people are ranked in order of power or importance
historians	people who study or write about history
immortality	the ability to live forever
irrigation ditches	ditches that help to supply water to areas of land
monuments	buildings or structures built to remember someone or something
myrrh	an expensive plant extract that is often used to make perfume
mythological	something that relates a traditional story or myth
peasants	poor land workers who belonged to the lowest social class
preserved	something that has been kept in its original state
priestesses	females who carry out religious actions or lead religious ceremonies
Seven Wonders of the Ancient World	seven of the most remarkable structures of the ancient world
society	a group of people who live together in a community
taxes	payments made to a country's government by the people who live there to help provide services
tribes	groups of people linked by family, social, religious or community ties

INDEX